The Other Woman

I0449242

The Other Woman

Will One Ever Be Enough?

Janie E. DeLaney

ISBN: 1-4196-6866-8
ISBN-13: 978-1419668661

Booksurge, LLC
7290 B Investment Drive
North Charleston, SC 29418

Visit www.booksurge.com to order additional copies.

The Other Woman

CONTENTS

ACKNOWLEDGMENTS

First and foremost I have to give God thanks for everything. He is my Alpha and Omega, without him I am nothing; it's because of him I've weathered many storms in my life. He was there in the beginning and he'll be there in the end. Thank you Jesus for being my all and all.

To my mom and dad, Robert L., Sr. and Doreatha DeLaney, because I am blessed to have wonderful parents like you, I never wanted for anything. I'd be lost without you.

Necee, my sister, my best friend; thank you for all the hours, days, and sleepless nights you sat up and talked with and to me, I couldn't be more blessed than to have a sister like you, you are truly a diamond in the rough, I will always love you.

My brother's Wade and Bobby, I love you guys, thanks for sharing your thoughts and insights with me, I truly appreciate and will forever cherish it.

Romona, Dwayne, Ashley, Joshua, Jeremiah, Jamon, Mario, and TaLayah, my nieces and nephews, always strive to be the best you can be, settle for nothing less. There's nothing you can't do, dream or become. Remember, "Faith is the substance of things hoped for, the evidence of things not seen." Hebrews 11:1 (NKJV).

Robin Harris, Debra Ridgeway, Aunt Sharon, Aunt Lula, Roz Coleman, Linda Hayes, Martina Tobarri-Kennedy,

Shawnda Sanders-Moultrie and many, many, many more. You guys were there for me when I needed you and for that I'll be forever grateful. For those of you I have not mentioned by name (because there are so many of you), please charge it to my head and not my heart.

To my son VJ who earned his angel wings over 16 years ago, I'll see you in the rapture; your mom is doing ok, my "little guy" who was gone before I knew it, and my baby girl Jazmyne E. Summers, you are my reason for living. God has big plans for you. You are destined for great things, always put and keep God first and everything else will be added unto you.

FOREWORD

I have known Janie E. DeLaney for more than sixteen years and it is indeed a pleasure to finally see her book completed. She hits home with some of the stories that she shares with her readers. I hope everyone that reads this book enjoys it as much as I did.

LT. R. Harris

Introduction

Cheaters have been around since the beginning of time and they're not going anywhere anytime soon. There are numerous books, articles, talk shows, radio personalities, and always tons of conversations going on about cheaters. There's even a television show with the same name.

"Everybody's doing it" or so the saying goes, but the truth is, everybody's not doing "it." Cheaters come in all shapes, sizes, nationalities, and income brackets.

Some people cheat for the chase, thrill, or excitement, while others cheat because they say what one partner won't do for them, another one will, and then again, some cheat just for the hell of it.

All in all, you will come across some people that are not willing to compromise their integrity for a rendezvous of any sort. There are various reasons and excuses people use and come up with to justify why they cheat.

Sometimes a person knows or has a feeling that they're being cheated on and at other times, they're none the wiser.

Take what you will from the stories I'm about to share with you. You may be able to relate to, know of someone, or have gone through something similar.

Janie E. DeLaney

I dedicate this book to all women, especially the women who had an impact in my life. For those of you that endured and persevered I admire you. Because of you, I will strive to be the best me that I can be. "In quietness and in confidence shall be your strength." Isaiah 30:15. "A gracious woman retains honor." Proverbs 11:16. "Who can find a virtuous woman? For her worth is far above rubies. Her children will rise up and call her blessed; Charm is deceitful and beauty is passing, but a woman who fears the Lord, she shall be praised." Proverbs 31:10-11; 28; 30

Chapter One

Cheaters

A= Absolute Cheaters

B= Basic Cheaters

C= Classical Cheaters

When does a man ever need a reason to cheat? Never. Then why does he? Because he wants to. A man that will cheat just for the hell of it is an absolute cheater. An absolute cheater is one who has a good home life. He has a loving and giving wife who assists him in taking care of the household, and a nurturer to their children. They live in a nice home, owns more than one car, finances are good, and last but not least, they have a GREAT sex life. You say to yourself, "Damn and he still cheats?" The painful truth is YES, he does.

There is no excuse of his wife not doing what he wants her to do at home or in bed, he's just greedy. An older woman once told me, "My mother said if you're not pleasing your man in the way he wants you to, he'll find someone else that will." That's a damn lie, you can please him all you want, and he, the "absolute cheater" is going to cheat anyway. That same woman that claimed she was a freak (anything goes) in bed for her man found out that doing everything her man wanted her to do sexually with him didn't do a damn thing for her. Not only did this man cheat on her, he had a child with the woman he had the affair with. One of whom his wife raised as her own along with their three children.

Another thing an absolute cheater won't do is, take money out of their household to wine and dine or spend on another woman. Dinner and a movie you say? That's nothing, but ask an absolute cheater to pay rent, mortgage, a car payment, or some other type of major bill and see how quick they stop calling. Try it, you'll see. They will come to your house or apartment, hell; they'll come to wherever you're footing the bill for a free piece of ass. It sounds harsh I know, but it's true.

"I'm not trying to leave home," Is one of the first things an absolute cheater will tell you. He really isn't trying to leave or get kicked out; he says this to a woman to get her reaction to see how far that particular woman will let him go. With some women it's a relationship, oh excuse me, a "sexsationship" that can last anywhere from a few months to several years. For the most part, an absolute cheater will most likely be involved with a married woman, simply because he figures she doesn't want any strings attached and they could split the cost of the tryst (most of the time). Be weary when you, the other woman, notice that you're footing most of the rendezvous bills. It can and has happened. That can be quite costly and incredibly ugly!

When an absolute cheater hooks up with a single woman, he'd better watch out!! Two things an absolute cheater can't stand is being cheated on or getting caught. Imagine that! These men have their wives and still want other women on the side and for the most part they do.

When a single woman threatens to tell the wife about the affair or ends up getting pregnant, the absolute cheater is either forced to tell the wife before the other woman does and risk losing everything he has, or string the other woman along long enough so if she does make good on her threat he can prepare his wife so they can decide what to do. Either way, that gives the wife the opportunity to decide if she wants to stay or if she's going to kick him out. Although in most cases the wife usually ends up leaving simply because the cheater refuses to leave and she doesn't want to go through the emotional rollercoaster that she feels she's been subjected to.

Another kind of single woman that participates in this kind of behavior with an absolute cheater that he sometimes fall for is known as a care giver; they take care of these men. Literally! From paying their bills to giving them money and experimenting in any sexual desires or fantasy they might have or express to have. She believes EVERYTHING he says, regardless to how unbelievable it sounds. She will stop doing whatever she's involved with to appease him at any given moment. She better not think twice about getting a man of her own, because that would send the absolute cheater into a rage. Why would it, if he's got his wife at home? Because he's gotten use to this woman pampering him, catering to his every need, and doing things on his terms; and to lose that to another man is truly unacceptable to him. He wants his wife and his mistress/girlfriend too. Thus one woman is not enough.

The basic cheater is one that cheats just for the sport of it. Yes, it's a sport to them, no feelings involved and no emotional attachment whatsoever. These guys are the hit it and quit it cheaters and in some cases they'll forget it. One night stands are common for the basic cheaters. These guys are the ones to hook up with groupies. They're not looking for a steady relationship and if they happen to be in one, it's for security purposes only; a place to lay their head, a home cooked meal, and somewhere to wash their ass on a regular basis. When they don't have the stability or comfort of those things, they go from pillow to post and in most cases; they still live at home with momma.

A lot of times these are your "pretty" boys. They know they look good and they truly believe that's all they need. For the most part, their looks are all they have going for them. They're usually summer workers, sometimes they work and sometimes they don't. Keeping a job is not important to them as getting a woman, any woman to take care of them physically and financially; but too vain to want emotional support. The basic cheater prey on women that are vulnerable. They normally seek out the women with low-self esteem, the single women in clubs that travel in packs, the married woman who's husband is having an affair (the basic cheater usually know when a husband is cheating on his wife which makes the wife fair game to them).

A basic cheater doesn't want to spend any money at all. Ever! Hell, they never have any. They want to be kept. No worries, cares, responsibilities or strings attached. Don't ever entertain the thought of getting pregnant by one of these men. The first thing that will come out of a basic cheaters mouth is "that baby in not mine and I want a blood test"; "you need to have an abortion"; or "how could you let something like that happen?" Yes, once that happens, they will want nothing to do with you. It doesn't matter if you were taking care of them, you betrayed them by trying to trap or get them to stay with you by getting pregnant on purpose (of course). After all, you're supposed to be the one on protection.

While the absolute cheater doesn't want anyone to know about you, a basic cheater will tell a friend of a friend of a friend about you so they can pass you around. Then you end up with a reputation. "She's like a door knob, everybody gets a turn." And the sign we hear about on the wall in the men's bathroom, "for a good time, call _____." When a basic cheater feels a person he is seeing has been seeing someone else besides him, he puts that woman through a series of tests.

Listen up ladies, these are some of the things he will do. Yes, this has happened to a woman that's why I'm letting you know. For all you men, I'm telling it and I'm telling it ALL. All I know, have seen, heard of, or been through.

A man will ask you to fix him a certain meal (if you don't have what he asks for, then you better go to the nearest grocery store and get it); he will tell you he's coming over (on more than one occasion) but NEVER show up; he'll ask you to buy him something (clothes, shoes, cologne, jewelry, etc.); take him somewhere; pay his cell phone bill; or perform oral sex on demand. Rest assure he's not testing you to see if you're marriage material (remember, they're not looking for a steady girlfriend, they're looking for a steady fool. He simply wants to see if he's got you! If you don't do any of those things for him, he'll accuse you of seeing someone else or he'll say you don't love him. For those of you that are strong willed and strong minded, walk away. For those of you that are not...well, I guess you'll just have to keep on keeping on until you can no longer do those things, take and pass those tests, or just get fed up.

I want to share this story of a basic cheater with you, and then I'll fill you in on the classical cheater.

I'll call this basic cheater Lonnie. Lonnie is not what one would call an ooo la la. Hell, he's not even an ooo. To make a long story longer he met a young lady by the name of Lori at a night club. I don't know what Lonnie saw in Lori to convince him that she would be the one he sinks his claws into. These two have been involved for over 3 ½ years and Lori has no clue as to where Lonnie lives. She has no physical address or home number to where she can reach him. According to Lonnie, they've never had a relationship, but let Lori tell it, and they're making plans to get married.

During the entire give a little, take a little relationship Lonnie never once bought Lori anything. Lonnie on the other hand has received expensive jewelry (e.g. several watches and a few fine rings), a few cell phones, (he's got to have the latest there is), clothes (e.g. Armani suits, name brand this name brand that), and shoes (Stacy Adams finest, Nike). As if that wasn't enough, she also makes his car payments, pay his rent, and gives him spending money. Damn! He hit the jackpot didn't he? Yes he did. Can you say cha ching? Lonnie has Lori trained, just as an owner has a puppy or dog. When he says jump, she says how high and where? Lonnie would tell (not ask, but tell) Lori to cook him something to eat and she'd get up or stop what she's doing to cook for him. She would never cook for herself, but the minute he asks for anything, she jumps up and does it immediately and it doesn't matter what time of day or night it is.

He would call her throughout the night to make sure she's at home so she wouldn't catch him in the street with someone else. We're all familiar with this kind of phone call, but for some reason, Lori truly believes Lonnie is calling to check up on her and her well being. Whenever they go out somewhere, he would never go to her house to pick her up unless they're going on a shopping spree for him. They would always meet somewhere (anywhere, as long as he didn't have to pick her up). If they go out to eat, they drive separate cars (keep in mind she makes his car payments from time to time), and he makes sure that they meet when and where it's convenient for him.

Lori goes for weeks at a time without seeing Lonnie. That is more than one clue that clearly states he's either married or living with someone. He would always be sure to call her on paydays. Yes, he knew when she got paid because she not only told him when she got paid, but how much. When he would finally go to see her, it would be late at night so nobody would see him. Hell, it's dark, he's dark-skinned, so who would know?

Whenever she wants to do something or go somewhere special (and she's paying), he frequently has an excuse to miss the event. He'll say he's tired, sleepy, sick, has a business trip, or he just doesn't show up. This has happened more than once and on more than one occasion. Lori believes ANYTHING and EVERYTHING that Lonnie tells her. After securing her trust, she's convinced herself to believe whatever he says. What's worse, she tries to convince everyone else to believe what he says as well! No can do girlfriend. Not when he leaves tell tale signs and clues as big as a pimple on someone's face.

He would tell her that's he's coming to see her and she'd get all dolled up for him and before you know it, several hours have passed and still no Lonnie. No matter how many no shows he pulled, she would always go through the same routine of getting ready and dolled up for him just in case he would show up.

Lonnie has proven beyond the shadow of a doubt that he has no intentions of building a life or future with Lori. Sure, he'll continue to spend her money and control every aspect of her life, but you can rest assure, he will not marry her. How could he, it's believed he's already married. Marrying Lori would make him a bigamist now wouldn't it?

Our classical cheaters are usually married. Unlike absolute cheaters, the classical cheaters home life is ok for the most part, but like the basic cheater, they care little or nothing about the other women they get involved with. They too try to hook up with someone who wants no strings attached although they've been known to fall for a few outside women themselves.

These cheaters have their wives and several other women on the side. What they don't get from one woman, they get from the other. What does that mean you say? He may love the way one woman cooks, how another one looks, which one is more adventurous in the bedroom, who strokes his ego to his liking and satisfaction, and who tends to be more attentive to his needs. All together these attributes make up their perfect woman. When they don't want to see these qualities in one woman, that's their excuse (that's not a reason) to have an affair. Oh, they come up with so many excuses its unreal. The oldest ones I've ever heard are "she made me turn to another woman" or "she pushed me into another woman's arms." Ok, if that's true, when he turns to that other woman, what makes him go to yet another woman? I said it before and I'll say it again, GREED. (Thus, one woman is not enough?)

The classical cheater is the one that will tell you, that he knows you're not going to tell anybody about the fling or affair that you're having with him, because you have too much class or you don't seem to be the kind of person that would run your mouth and tell other people your business, and you appear to know how to be discreet.

Let me translate that for you: "I hope you don't tell anybody that I'm having sex with you, because I don't want anyone to know. Besides that, you wouldn't want anyone to know you're fooling around with a married man would you? As much as I enjoy and look forward to having sex with you, I really would rather you keep it between us, so please don't tell anyone. I'd appreciate it."

If a man tells you that or anything close to it, run. Run far, far, far away from him and don't look back!!

Sure there's more than the absolute, basic and classical cheaters out there, I just wanted to share a few of the characteristics of the A, B, C, cheaters with you, which are the most common.

One woman will never be enough for some men. These men run and run and run and then their either too tired to run anymore or their just no good for anybody. That's when they decide they want to spend the rest of their lives at home with their wives. For some it's too late because some of their wives have continued living their lives; they got use to not having their husbands around, and for those that were fortunate to have their wives put their lives on hold until they were done running around with all those other women.........well, that's another story.

Chapter Two

Oliver & Olivia

The Way We Were

Oliver and Olivia have been married for 40 years. This couple has a good family life. They have six children, two boys and four girls. They live in a nice house and drive nice cars. They appear to be an ideal couple, but looks can really be deceiving.

Imagine the shock, disbelief, gossip, pain and hurt this entire family went through when a rumor stated that Oliver had one child by another woman No, we're not just talking one or two outside of the marriage kids, were talking an entire family. The initial rumor stated there was one child by another woman but there were actually six other kids all by the same woman. WOW!

I wondered where on earth did a married man with six kids, find time to go out and make another family of six. The answer is simple, he was extremely creative and didn't use protection, thus he not only went out and has all these other kids behind Olivia's back, he was also putting her at risk for disease! Forget about her feelings, he was beyond caring at this point.

Olivia heard rumors throughout her marriage about the affair and the outside kids, but it was never something she had proof of and when she asked Oliver about it, he would flat out deny it; all of it. Oliver's lies did go on for a little over 17 years until one day, one of the alleged outside kids needed blood after being in a car accident. Lo' and behold when it came down to the wire, Oliver turned out to be the child's father! His whole world came tumbling down.

The kids he has with Olivia (his wife) distanced themselves from him. They could not believe this man that they called daddy and looked up to could do something like this to their mother. What was he thinking? He wasn't. What was it about this other woman that had him going back? Stupidity? Leisure sex? Oliver had a good life with his wife Olivia and their children. Greed and the need to have more than one woman fascinated him, but did he have to go out there and make all those babies? I think not. What was the purpose? There is none. Bottom line, Oliver just didn't care enough about his wife and their family.

When Olivia asked him, he should've told the truth. If the outside child wasn't in the car accident, I wonder if he would've ever told.....Probably NOT!

And the other woman; I guess she was just too stupid. Yes, I said stupid. You would think after having the first baby and Oliver is still with Olivia he isn't planning on leaving his wife regardless of what he told that other woman, but she goes on to have five more kids. And you guessed it; Oliver and Olivia are still together.

Sure people wondered, talked about and asked, "How on earth can Olivia live with him after all he's done? He put her at risk for disease, tearing his family apart, subjected them to more gossip and whispers." Where were his morals? If he had any they must have been suppressed or made dormant.

I'm not sure if Oliver has a relationship with any of his kids, Lord knows he's got enough, but he and Olivia stayed together. Fortunately for Oliver, Olivia was a church going woman who always prayed; her faith in God never wavering. There were times she could be heard weeping and at other times she seemed down, but she remained humble with her head held high and her dignity intact. It takes a strong woman to endure all those things and maintain some sense of self. One would have to be to stay with a man after all of that. God Bless you Olivia.

Chapter Three

Lorenzo & Barbara

Marriage of Convenience

Lorenzo and Barbara, the couple that seem to have everything but a marriage!! These two have been married for 30+ years and they have three girls and one boy. Theirs is a story of...hmm, I don't know what you'd call it, so I'll just tell their story.

Lorenzo use to be a stripper. That's where he met Barbara (at the strip club where he worked). After dating for three years, they got married. I didn't know strippers had serious dates, instead of one night stands or group settings. A monogamous relationship, right. Oh boy, why did they do that? They weren't married two years before Lorenzo starting having explicit affairs with many women.

He had seven kids with three different women. One of the women Lorenzo had an affair with started calling Barbara to tell her about the affair and when Barbara confronted him, he denied his affair (do they all deny it)? What a surprise. This other woman was so bold, she would drive pass Barbara and Lorenzo's house. She knew where they lived because she followed him home after one of their many rendezvous. That wasn't enough for this woman, she wanted Lorenzo for herself. She went so far as to have one of her friends take pictures of her and Lorenzo on an outing and she sent them in the mail to Barbara, who then figured she had confirmation/proof that what this woman told her about her husband was true.

Barbara left Lorenzo, but the funny thing is Lorenzo dropped the other woman who caused Barbara to leave him like yesterday's news. Sure, Elaine, the other woman was distraught and mad at herself because she had Lorenzo on the side, but now she doesn't have him at all. That picture cost her the side item she was getting on a regular basis.

Lorenzo had plans (big plans). He started pursuing Barbara again. He was sending her flowers on her job, sent her cards in the mail and left love notes on the windshield of her car.

After performing those acts of kindness, he asked her out to dinner and she gladly accepted. Barbara was on top of the world; being wined and dined by Lorenzo for the entire world to see. Lorenzo continued to do these things until he finally convinced Barbara to give him another chance. Don't ask me how, I don't know. One thing I do know for sure is, we know what we have (at least we think we do), but we don't know what we'll get. Well, she did give him another chance and boy oh boy was she ever sorry she did that. As soon as she and Lorenzo got back together, he was back in the street again, this time bolder than ever. He wasn't sneaking around anymore; he was out in the open with his infidelity. He truly doesn't care nor does he consider Barbara's or his family feelings at all. When he displays this kind of behavior, it's totally disrespectful, distasteful, and completely unacceptable, but if Barbara's fine with it, who am I or any other woman to knock it? Some of us have a problem with it because other men expect us to be submissive and to accept this type of behavior and the minute we decide we're not going to, that's when it poses a problem.

One never knows why a person stays in relationships like that, but the questions never change. Why does she stay with him knowing he's having an ongoing affair? Its one thing to suspect your spouse or significant other is having an affair (ongoing or not), but to know he's having an affair, that's really bad!! When he's not with her, is he with one of those other women? Which one? The questions go on and on but those are just a few. And let's face it, for some of us, our peace of mine is non-negotiable. Desires, needs, and wants we all have, but at what price or cost are we willing to pay?

Although Lorenzo and Barbara stayed together, they live total separate lives. One would say it's a marriage of convenience, a business arrangement with benefits, or the one we all know of, "it's cheaper to keep her." Keep your head up Barbara, let go and let God.

Chapter Four

Erik & Octavia

Material Mate

Erik and Octavia married 32 years, three kids, two girls and one boy. Erik and Octavia were not high school sweethearts; they were sandbox sweethearts (preschool).

Octavia is naive as they come. Erik has been cheating on her for forever. He still does.

Erik has been seen with several different women and when Octavia was told about it, she said, "My husband won't cheat on me." I thought; oh my goodness, what spell does Erik have on her? I don't ever want a man to have that kind of spell on me.

Octavia is the kind of woman that could see Erik's ass going up and down, side to side, back and forth with a woman beneath him and he would tell her, "it's not what it looks like; your eyes are deceiving you." And she would believe him.

Did I mention that Erik has four other kids with three other women? Well he does and they're not with Octavia (I guess that throws the "my husband won't cheat on me" theory is out the window).

Octavia cherishes things; material things; house, cars, home accessories, etc. But while she's cherishing those things, her husband is having the time of his life. What does she care; she's surrounded by the materialism she's never had in her life. Sometimes she acts as if she's anti-social, but if there's a function where she can show off what she's got, she's there! She loves comparing what she has to what someone else has. Please don't go out and purchase a house or a car, because she'd want to know how you got it? Could you afford it, what did it cost you? Yes, it's sad, but that's how she is. Hell her whole family is like that (down to the children). Instead of them being happy for someone who has good fortune and is able to get the (material) things they want in life, they straight up hate on them. I bet you know people like that don't you? Sure you do, we all do. It may not be as bad as Octavia and her bunch, but they're out there.

While she's wondering who's got what, where they got it from, how much it cost, and how the person is paid for it, Erik is out womanizing one woman after another. He's not too sneaky about it either; depending on who he's seeing at the time is how he determines how discreet he will be. If the woman is well known (after being with a few other men or too many men, some of these women get reputations), he doesn't want anyone to know that he's seeing that particular woman. Although it seems as though Erik has cut back on going out. Hmm, could he be changing from his cheating ways? Not!! He's probably tired and worn out. It happens. At least Octavia has all the "things" she wants.

Besides being materialistic, Octavia is also color struck. She's extremely fascinated by light-skinned people. I believe she wish she was light-skinned, I would say to her, "be thankful and grateful for all that you have including the complexion bestowed upon you". Since Erik gives her all the things she wants materialistically, I think she overlooks his indiscretions. But hey, if that's what works for them, so be it. I say to Octavia, "sorry it's you and glad it isn't me."

Chapter Five

Leroy & Vera

What a Man

L eRoy and Vera. This couple has been married for 29 years; they have four kids, two boys and two girls.

Have you ever heard of loving someone too much? Well this is believed to be the story of these two. LeRoy loved his wife so much that she didn't want for anything. LeRoy made sure Vera had all she ever wanted.

This is a man that is not ashamed of showing his affection in public. He'd hold her hand (when she would let him), open the door for her when she got into or out of the car, and the first thing he'd do when he got home after a long day at work was kiss her on the cheek and ask her how was her day. Did Vera appreciate it? I would say NO. She would never give LeRoy the time of day. The only time she seemed to want to give him any attention is when she thought someone else was. Talk about your tug-of-war yo-yo type of love. She even had the nerve to tell him he was being overbearing, smothering her almost. Oh, oh. That was all he needed to hear. From that moment on, he no longer held her hand in public; they didn't go to too many places together anymore and when she attempted to be affectionate he'd back off. This was clearly a case of pushing someone away.

LeRoy did not hang out with the fellas', go club jumping, or bar hopping.

He was a home body. He stayed at home, took care of and provided for his family. I don't know what Vera wanted, but when she made that statement to LeRoy about him smothering her, he started going out. He didn't go out every night, mostly on the weekends.

He was still a good dad and provider for his family, he just sought affection from another woman that was more than willing and happy to oblige, outside of his smothering marriage. Damn, talk about being hurt. Before long, Vera wanted to spend more time with him and she realized she missed being smothered, but guess what? That's right, he was not available.

Not for her anyway. She didn't realize what she had until it was no longer there. Isn't that the case with most of us? Yeah, it is. So the saying goes, "you don't miss your water 'til your well runs dry".

LeRoy could no longer stay with Vera because she didn't appreciate him or what he did for their family and although he continued to provide for them, he went home to live with his mother and that is where he remains to this present day.

I believe all women want their men to be attentive. So what if it's a bit much, I know it's better than no attention at all. Ladies if you've got a man that is more than willing to be affectionate in public or private, embrace it, hell embrace him. I've heard the stories of some men not being affectionate, attentive, or showing any kind of emotion. Some of them are down right distant and non-communicative. Now who wants that? I'd be the first to raise my hand and say, "not me." All I can say to Vera is............You will never find another man like LeRoy in this lifetime. NEVER!

Chapter Six

Landon & Unique

The Ideal Couple

Landon and Unique. Oh to look at this couple one would think, "ooo, I want a marriage like that." If you ever heard these sayings, "All that glitters isn't gold, and the grass looks greener on the other side" then you would come to appreciate what you have.

This couple is known as the "cute" couple. Unique has the looks of what society stereotypes as that of a runway model and Landon is quite the dapper one with his chiseled chin and bronze complexion. These two are what one would call the "Hollywood Couple" of the common folk. They were married just a little over 21 years with six kids, three boys and three girls. This dynamic duo of a couple lives in a nice six bedrooms, 4 bathrooms, and three car garage all brick home. Their back yard has a gazebo and an in ground pool.

Now having all that and more, Landon cheated on Unique anyway. Yes they have a good sex life, but he like so many other men, he wanted his wife and his other woman on the side. It's one thing to have an affair or two, hell, maybe even three or more (as he had), but come on, you don't have to make babies with these women. Unique found out about Landon early on into the marriage and yes, she stayed anyway.

I don't know why and she didn't offer any explanations although she did say she felt like a fool for staying but she didn't have the strength to leave. I know some of you are reading this story and saying to yourself, "I would've left", hell, when she told me about it, I thought "that crap would've given me just enough strength to leave" even if it was just for a few months to clear my head, get my thoughts together and execute some kind of plan for my future and the future of the kids.

When a woman becomes accustomed to a particular lifestyle that she's built with a man as Unique has with Landon, they tend to overlook quite a few of their husbands indiscretions. No matter how big or small.

It doesn't matter what whispers or gossip people will say about them, not as long as their living in that big house, driving that fancy car, getting their nails and hair done on a regular basis and last but not least, they're still the wife and that other woman is just that. The other woman!

Unique knows of this other woman, she's even seen her a few times, but her business is not with this woman, it's with Landon. Unique doesn't know what Landon is telling this other woman. He could be telling her he's staying with Unique for the kids, or they stay in the same house but they don't sleep in the same bed, she would take everything he owns if he leaves her now, she may fall apart and he doesn't want his kids to resent him.

The excuses are endless, but it would take Landon to nip it in the bud, not Unique. Now if the other woman sees that Landon isn't trying to leave home and he makes up one excuse after another, she can then leave Landon alone, but that has not happened, so I guess this affair will be on going until somebody decides it's time to move on.

There will be no winners or losers, just individuals with broken heart and lives. I know what would put a twist on things. What if Unique and the woman end up dumping Landon and being the best of friends? NOT!

Hang in there Unique, after all, you're his wife, you live in the big house, drive the fancy luxurious cars, and you have his kids (oops, so does she). Oh well, it was worth a try wouldn't you say?

Why do people get married? The reasons are numerous and endless, why they stay together in a lifeless and loveless marriage is beyond me.

You go Unique, because the bottom line is you are the wife!

Chapter Seven

Ernest & Anita

A Leopard Never Changes Its Spots

Here's a story of a married man by the name of Ernest, who's been cheating on his wife for more than 15 years.

Ernest is a salesman, so in his line of work, he's always in and out of town or working late hours (so he says). He is a creature of habit as all men are.

One day Ernest left his cell phone home and while he was out, his wife not only answered his phone when it rang, she also listened to his voicemail messages. One of the messages just happened to be from one of his many lovers (his wife didn't know a thing about). This is the message the other woman left for Ernest. "Ernest, I haven't heard from you in a few days, what's going on? I really enjoyed the time we spent together; I wish it didn't have to end. Remember what I told you. I will leave my husband and you leave your wife and we could be happy together." After listening to that message, Ernest's' wife hit the roof, and all hell broke loose. She started throwing his clothes and other belongings out the window. She then wanted him to produce receipts of where he stayed while he was on the road, where he ate, and any stops he may have made on the way. It was a task that Ernest could not fulfill, simply because he never paid for anything. He's the kind of (absolute) cheater you would never want to get involved with. He's truly a taker and he will take as long as you are giving. A good example of that is if he's in a familiar place, where he might be recognized, he would ask that particular woman he's with to foot the bill and he would either reimburse her or go half. He does neither. Before you know it, he owes you over $100+. Watch out now!

No, he can't meet you anywhere if it's not within a 5-10 mile radius for him. Now if you happen to be in his neck of the woods, he'll be more than happy to meet you, after all it has to be by his rules, done his way, or only at HIS convenience.

Needless to say, after Anita cooled off, she kept a leash on Ernest. It worked for a little while, but a leopard never changes it spots. Anita did tell him if he didn't straighten up, she would kick him out.

Now you would think Ernest would have dropped the other woman like yesterday's news, but he didn't. He's gotten a little wiser at being discreet with that particular woman.

Ernest's story doesn't end there. There have been several other women he's had an affair with and still has on going affairs with some of them. One of the other women that he got involved with told him he had too many female friends. He politely told her, "If my wife doesn't have a problem with it, why should you? You're not the first woman to tell me that I have too many female friends. I always tell a woman from the start, that I'm not trying to leave my wife (or home), this way they'll know up front what they're getting into."

Now isn't that a bunch of crap? Yes it is! You have this damn man that clearly makes the sub-title of this book "will one ever be enough?" an understatement. He's selfish, greedy as hell, and don't give a damn about anybody but himself! One of the women he was involved with says he's a user and doesn't like to spend any money, and only wants to spend time with you when it's convenient for him.

Not only that, he had rules. Imagine that, a married man with rules for the other woman and wanting to dominate the entire relationship (if that's what one wants to call it).

He said he didn't like or want to French kiss because he had a bad kissing experience in the past, he didn't like to perform oral sex, but enjoyed having it done to him, service me, but I won't service you type deal. He even had the nerve to say he's NEVER done that before, not even with his wife. To put the icing on the cake, he asked the other woman could he do her in the ass. Yes, he wanted to have anal sex with this woman. She told him to stay home, do his wife in the ass, and don't come out to play, because he doesn't know how too. After being told that, he no longer talks to this particular woman, but she is one of the one's who just didn't want to put up with some other woman's husband.

This man would get mad (down right angry) if everything didn't go his way.

Some women don't want to get out of situations such as that, some are in too deep to get out, and some just don't know how to get out, and as sad as it sounds and might be, some women just feel they're not worthy. This could stem from low self-esteem, or just believing that because some man told them so. It's times like these when you know that old saying; "it's easier said than done" seems to hold true.

Believe me when I tell you, if you have faith and self-love, you can and will get through it, no matter how bad or hard it seems at the moment.

In case you're wondering what's up with Ernest, we're just waiting for him to get busted!! If he doesn't get caught (with his naked ass up in the air). He's still up to no good so it's bound to happen or come out sooner or later (unless he stops cheating..... like that will happen). It remains to be seen.

Chapter Eight

Ike & Aniah

Not Meant To Be

How could this happen to me? I did everything a wife would do for her husband. I cooked; cleaned, reared our children and I worked to help out financially. I was his friend, his lover, and his wife.

All of that came to a screeching halt, and my life and the life of our children were changed forever. My husband had an affair!! Truth of the matter is, I never suspected a thing. We got along fine; we had a good home life, bills were paid on time, and we did things as a family.

He comes from a large family, four brothers and four sisters, so when he would go to visit them (or so he would say), I had no reason to believe he wasn't going to do just that. Then one day one of his relatives told me he was seeing another woman that lived in the same building as they did!! Hmm, that explains all those visits to his relative's home.

From that moment on, I always suspected him of cheating when he left the house, (didn't matter if he was or not, the seed had been planted). After dealing with the news his relative gave me, I confronted him (no, I didn't tell him who told me, I just asked him), "are you having an affair?" He hit the roof, and started yelling and cursing (a sure sign of guilt). "Who told you that?" I told him, "that's not important, just answer the question."

You see, when a man gets busted (or has been found out), he loses control, jumps on the defensive, and the worse thing he can ever do to make it worse (or even try to justify it, is to accuse you of the exact same thing you just found out about him). As horrible as this may sound, it's true. Men will and have done that. My husband did.

At that point, I decided my marriage was over. No, I didn't leave right away, nor did I share this information with my husband. As a matter of fact, I stayed for a few years (to get myself, my children, and finances in order). I continued to cook, clean, and take care of the household. I say that to let you know...Men are creatures of habit, so when they change up on things that they would normally do, WATCH OUT!

Some of the signs to look out for......his working hours suddenly changed, he has to work late, go out of town, has late meetings, and shows little or no interest in being intimate, etc... the reasoning is never ending—and they can get quite creative, so watch out for that too.

I informed my husband from the beginning of our marriage, that there would not be an outsider that will destroy us; it would have to be one of us. And lo and behold, he finally did it. It wasn't so much his affair that destroyed the marriage; it was his constant ongoing verbal and mental abuse. That kind of abuse will either make you snap or give you enough will power to just walk away.

I left everything. I knew all the material things I was leaving behind I could replace, but my peace of mind is non-negotiable.

I've heard the stories of women having mental or nervous break downs because of what a man put them through. I was not going to be a statistic, not in that category anyway.

If a man doesn't want you, let him go. Sure it's easier to say than do, but if you're going to lose sleep, your sanity, sense of self, or anything else that means something to you, let him GO! I'm not saying your feeling will go away over night, but you'll have to move on. If you don't time won't stop for you and the world will keep on going.

Should a man tell you that no one else will want you, guess what he's trying to do? He's trying to keep you from moving on and being happy. In the end, you're responsible for your happiness. You can enjoy being happy with someone, just try not to lose yourself in the meantime.

Some women won't be strong or brave enough to get out of a "terrible" or "bad" marriage. Some will stay just for the sake of saying they stayed married this or that many years, or they fear what people or relatives might say if the marriage falls apart or is dissolved.

For those women that choose to stay, I won't knock you, but you shouldn't stay and complain about your husbands' whereabouts. The two just don't marry up.

Chapter Nine

Confronting The Other Woman

L adies, ladies, ladies. Listen UP!!! If you ever (and I mean EVER) think about confronting another woman regarding your husband (boyfriend, or significant other), please have your facts together and be a woman about it, NOTHING less.

The fact of the matter is, you may or may not know the woman that your man is messing, fooling around or having an affair with, and that story about the wife being the last to know...., well, I beg to differ. You see, women have this thing called intuition. Oh it's real. It's when we get a feeling about something, especially when it comes to our man and we just can't quite put our finger or hand on it.

Long before we hear of our husbands or man cheating on us, we already suspect it just by the way he acts or reacts to something; it can be as simple as a spoken word or a particular situation. As I stated earlier, men are creatures of habit, so when they try to change the slightest thing after years of continuity a bell rings or a light comes on. Talk about an aha moment.

When confronting the other woman, the confrontation will either be verbal; by phone, a face to face meeting in a public place, a letter in the mail, or an email.

I'm going to share a personal experience of being confronted. Specifically, here are a couple of emails a woman sent to someone (her husband use to date in high school). Please note that these two emails she sent are EXACTLY as originally sent (unedited for authenticity, bad grammar and typos left in); with the exception of the sender, receiver, and anyone copied names being changed.

I intentionally left the emails in their original context to let women know this is NOT something you'd send to another woman, especially if you think or suspect your husband is involved with her in any way, shape, form or fashion.

If you decide to send an email, make sure you dot the I's (i), cross the T's (t), and perform a spell and grammar check. This proud wife not only seems to have internal issues, but she also goes on to say she has a Master's Degree and I quote "analyzing simple and pathetic people." When you read these emails you will come to the conclusion that her degree is not in English Composition although she really never specifically states what her degree is in.

If you decide to use the email method, proof your work first. Hell, have someone to edit it for you, especially if you're going to make a statement about your educational background. I'm still baffled as to why she put that in there in the first place. Hmm, go figure. Just remember this.......commit nothing to paper that you wouldn't want anyone else to know about. If you're sending an email out of anger, remember once you hit the send command it's gone and you will have no control as to where it ends up. You can however, compose an email and then delete it. Without further ado here are the emails:

(Email #1)

Hi Jay Dear,

Can you forward your husband's e-mail address to me so that I can e-mail him since you can't seem to get over mine? Or better yet, give me your home phone number (I already have your cell) so I can call him. Hey, maybe we can swap? What do you think? Both you and Cain (my husband) are pathetic. It's been 16 years and you are still not over it. You are being played for a fool. Cain will e-mail you and play with your mind; but he will never be caught DEAD with you in public because as he puts it, he would be too embarrassed to be seen with you (well um....we heard how you look these days...people do talk....and needless to say, well, you know....because you see yourself every day.) He will go to his grave claiming that he would never even call you because anyone that knows about it would think that he has lost his damn mind. Go out and get yourself some self-esteem because as one woman to another you are being played girlfriend. He is playing you dear I

can't explain it any clear than that. Cain' self-esteem is very low these days and you are merely the "thing" that he is using to make himself feel better about himself because no matter how he leads you on, you'll be there when he needs a should to cry or piss on. The times that he is contacting you, I'm giving him hell and that's what that's all about. Oh I guess that's where my "Master's Degree" comes in handy analyzing simple, pathetic, people who cant seem to move past Battery Creek High School. It was high school dear— both of you need to let it go. Or better yet, make yourselves happy and get together. He'll never take you outside but you'll have him to yourself:—) HOW BOUT THAT?
Sincerely,
THE ONE AND ONLY MRS CAIN......OOOPS, GUESS YOU ALREADY KNEW THAT.

To ensure that there would be no surprises, she copied both emails to her husband. The wife didn't stop there with her boldness and intellect, for she called Jay's cell phone three times that same day. When the wife spoke to Jay, she asked her, "Are you not over my husband?" Jay replied, "The question is, is your husband over me?" The wife started raising her voice telling Jay, "He's married to me!" Jay simply and quietly responded, "He sure is, so why the hell are you calling me?" Jay then ended the call by hanging up the phone. The next two calls she placed to Jay was answered by Jay's co-worker, Dolly. By this time a few of Jay's co-workers had read the emails and knew what was brewing and being that Jay was just informed that her Uncle Alvin had passed away, she was in no mood for anymore of Mrs. Cain's phone calls. Dolly politely told Mrs. Cain to take that Master's Degree she says she has and put it to good use.

The wife got Jay's cell phone number from one of Cain's email correspondence. She went so far as to send Jay an email using her husbands' email account to ask Jay for her home number. I guess she really thought she was dealing with someone that she labeled as simple and pathetic. She truly underestimated this one because she never got the number. The lesson here: Although one may obtain a Master's Degree, it doesn't teach you how to act.

This wife states that Jay and Cain (her husband) are pathetic, Jay is being played for a fool, and then she goes on to state that Cain will email and play with Jay's mind; but he will never be caught DEAD with her in public......Cain will go to his grave claiming he would never call Jay because anyone that knows about it would think he lost his damn mind. After reading this email, I believe the wife with the Master's Degree lost her damn mind!

Here's a kicker.......Go out and get yourself some self-esteem, because as one woman to another you are being played. How can Cain possibly be playing Jay if what the wife says in the above email is true? She goes on to say that Cain's self-esteem is very low these days (hmm, makes you wonder why)? And that Jay is merely the "thing" that Cain is using to make himself feel better because no matter how he leads her on, she will be there when he needs a shoulder (although she has should) to cry or piss on. Ouch, was that supposed to hurt?! And just how is Cain using Jay?

Ok, we're almost at the end of email #1. The times that he is contacting you, I'm giving him hell and that's what that's all about.

Reader(s), help me out here. Did I miss something or did this woman state that Cain (her husband) would be too embarrassed for anyone to know that he is in contact with Jay at all? Looks like the wife can use a little analyzing herself.

Was the wife crying out for help or what at the end of this email? Cain and Jay, both of you need to let go, or get together and make each other happy.

Be careful of what you say in the heat of anger and more so when you put it in writing. The tongue is a weapon and your words have a way of going out and around and then returning to you and bite you on the ass!! Cain will never take you outside Jay, but you'll have him all to yourself. Then she tops it off with a winking smiley face. How cute :—)?

Jay never responds to the first email, thus the reason for email number two. Because Jay didn't entertain Cain's wife, she called Jay boring. I truly believe all the things she wrote about Jay are true reflections of Mrs. Cain herself.

(Email #2)
Hey Boo (Oops—Pun Intended)!

I see you got my e-mail. Well I am just so VERY hurt that you don't want to talk to me—Cousin. Since we are regressing to BCHS days, that is what you signed in my memory book (that you were my cousin—remember?). Oh, you probably don't remember that. Maybe I'll scan it and send it to you. Oh, better yet—-I'll let my HUSBAND scan it and send it to you. HOW BOUT THAT?
Here are a few things you should keep in mind:
(A) I AM GOING TO CONTACT YOUR HUSBAND, could be today, tomorrow, next week or next year. Since you like mine so much, let's see how much I like yours.
(B) I've decided you are boring. I'll work on trying to contact your husband.

Love and hugs....Cain's wife :—).

Ok readers what do you think about those emails from the one and only Mrs. Cain? Initially she talks about her husband never being caught dead in public, too embarrassed to be seen with, and will go to his grave claiming he would never call Jay. Then in the same breath, she calls Jay and her husband Cain pathetic, informs Jay she's being played, used and led on. And what's with the statement (and I quote) "The times that he is contacting you." Now which is it, is he in contact with Jay or not? What woman in her right mind would tell another woman to get together with her husband and be happy? I know of no such woman.

I believe the words were sent out of anger. Angry with whom you say? I'd say she's angry at herself, for actually sending the emails and angry at her husband. Talk about putting somebody down to make yourself feel better.

In this life we're given a series of trials, tribulations, triumphs and defeat. Whatever the circumstance, consequence, or outcome may be, DON'T LOSE THE LESSON. EVER!

You never want to dog out your husband or man to another woman; don't call him out his name, belittle him, or put him down. It doesn't matter how mad you are or how mad you get. Tell him off if you're that angry. You never want to give another woman that kind of knowledge, insight, power, or ammunition.

Know that once you release such information, if it's true or not, it's released! To let another woman you think your husband may be involved with know what you think or feel about him, especially if it's negative is NEVER a good thing. So what if the person is being played, what do you care? Cain (her husband) and Jay did date in high school, so that's the "it" they're suppose to get over?

This wife clearly has esteem issues and she seems very angry. So much so, she wanted Jay to feel just as bad and as miserable as she did. The best remedy for an issue like this is to not respond. This is exactly what Jay did in this case.

The wife and Jay never had bad words, it's just that they both dated this man at different times; they were never friends, but they were cordial to one another. They did go to high school together. The wife is older than both Jay and Cain by a few years.

Cain and Jay have always been good friends and although the relationship ended, their friendship did not. I believe that is the biggest issue the wife has with this. Her husband may actually have genuine feelings for Jay and she knows it (intuition) and that's probably why she lashed out the way she did in both emails and those harassing phone calls, not to mention her tremendous and well known dislike for Jay.

This wife does not want her husband to be around Jay at all. Jay doesn't seem to know why since Cain's wife already said he wouldn't be caught dead with her, it would be too embarrassing, and she looks a mess or so people say. No, don't quite know what people she's talking about, but hey, he did marry her, so what's the problem?

Verbal confrontations are no better because they can escalate into something physical and the last time I checked; fighting over a man just isn't worth it. Nine times out of ten, he'll continue being with the both of you. And no chocolate (dark or vanilla) is that sweet or that good!

If you verbalize over the phone, you'd make yourself look and sound like a fool; simply because you don't know what your husband has told this other woman. The best thing that you can do is confront your husband/man, not the other woman.

If you feel you need to or just want to confront the other woman, don't.

Chapter Ten

In Conclusion

While you're reading this book and long after you've finished, you'll feel you know, are related to, went to school, work or are neighbors with anyone of the people/couples mentioned herein.

The cycle of the other woman will never end. I don't know all the signs, but here are just a few:

- If you're dating a man and you don't have his home number, a (legitimate) physical address, you've never been to his house or visited where he lives, chances are he's married or living with someone.
- His working hours suddenly changes.
- He has to work late (all the time).
- He has frequent out of town/business trips (unless he's a pilot or in a similar line of work, it's questionable).
- His pager (or cell phone) goes off during all hours of the night (and he's not a doctor, so he's not on call).
- He has little or no interest in being intimate (at all).

If you're married and you suspect your husband is cheating or having an affair, chances are he probably is. So no, you don't have to call Cheaters to confirm your suspicions. What you can do is ask him (sure, he'll more than likely lie about it or flat out deny it).

The oldest trick in the book (no, I don't know which book) is when a man starts an argument for no reason. This is where he will storm out of the house insisting that he needs to cool off, which is usually at o dark thirty in the morning or late at night.

Some women are ok with being the other woman. And like some men, they do it for the sport of it. The thrill or excitement of having another woman's husband gives them a euphoric high. They don't think about what would or could happen once the high wears off.

Just know that for every action there are consequences. For every woman that says no to a married man, there are two or more that will say yes and are more than willing to be the other woman.

For the women that say yes to these men, you can not start demanding to know his whereabouts, wanting him to spend more time with you, spending holidays or special occasions with you, and to call you from time to time. The list goes on and on, but the first thing you must remember is you are NOT the wife, you're the other woman. Now if you didn't know he was married......well Hell, look for the signs.

You may know or have known of someone that has been or is the other woman. You yourself maybe or might have been the other woman (knowingly or unknowingly) at some point and time. Whichever one of these categories you fall or fit into; because you do fit into one of them, you'll be able to relate to one or more of the stories you just read.

Although some situations have similarities, the individuals are different. After all is said and done, some wives will choose to stay and some will leave.

I said it before and I'll say it again, one woman will never be enough for some men. What some women can and will tolerate, others will not. What works best for some may not work for others. You have to decide and figure out what works BEST for YOU! Hopefully whatever you decide, you'll be wiser and have more understanding.

What happens when the wife cheats or has an affair? You'll have to read the next book to find out...................................

JANIE E. DeLANEY is a native Virginian born in Quantico and raised in Beaufort, South Carolina. She's a single mom to a loving teenage daughter. Janie is well traveled, and a veteran of the United States Navy. She is currently a Department of Defense employee on a high profile Army program. She is currently working on two other books as well as other projects.